To Pes, May the blessings of our friendship increase as ours. Linda

To Be Enough:
40 Attempts to Rest in Love

ISBN-13: 978-1985206540
ISBN-10: 1985206544
All scripture verses are quoted from the New International Version.

To my daughters.

LINDA STRUBE

There comes a day when you
start trusting your story
and believe you are truly loved.

Lent is time to walk toward a story that reminds
we are held from eternity.
It lets us take a journey together
practicing good health for our souls.
I call these exercises soul stretches.

These next 40 days each contain a meditation or poem,
a scripture, and a daily soul stretch challenge

Some days the soul stretch will ask you
to add something to your routine.
Others will ask you to take away something
that you've clung to.
Some days are easier than others.
Stick with it.
Lent is a journey designed to
return us to truth and
give our hearts room to breath.

Know I will be stretching right alongside you.
Simply, you are enough.

-Linda

Forward

One of my earliest memories of my mother Linda is attending Good Friday service with her in New Jersey. For my mother, it was the peak of her spiritual calendar. For me, Good Friday was a full day off from school, one of the first afternoons where jackets needn't be worn, where flowers were blooming and grass returning to our yard. The last place I wanted to be was a dark cathedral for a three-hour service, listening to 7 sermons. To occupy myself, I brought my coloring books and goldfish crackers while my mother listened intently. In grade school, I graduated to pencils and stickers. By the time I reached college, I found myself looking for my own candlelit cathedral to rest that Friday afternoon.

Year after year, this became our ritual, starting Lent with ashes on our forehead and ending it with lilies. My mother taught me that Lent was a time to pause, to focus on soulful work, to let go of things that weighed me down and add things that lifted me up.

Our hope is for you to find ways to do the same. Give yourself 40 days to let your guard down and let yourself be loved. It will only take a few moments.

We promise not to keep you for hours.

- Jennifer Strube, Editor + Soul Stretcher

LENTEN MEDITATIONS

1. Come
2. To Be Enough
3. To Be With Yourself
4. In Praise of Beauty
5. Finding the Romance
6. Following Mystery
7. To Play
8. On Friendship
9. Taste and See
10. Embrace the Beyond
11. To Passion
12. Return to Belief
13. Prayer
14. To Listen
15. Learn from Nature
16. Worship
17. Music of Praise
18. I Don't Know How
19. Discovery
20. To Grieve
21. To Weep
22. The Practice of Honesty
23. Pain and Pleasure

To Be Enough:
40 Attempts to Rest in Love

1. Come

Come with your skinned knees, false eyelashes, grown beards, and fossils. Lay down your weapons and gadgets and keyboards. Rise from the hayloft, you laborers of dirt, and surrender your sweat. Come in striped-colored ties and sturdy black briefcases and stand with the pioneer choruses from lore and dream. Here is no time nor space, rich nor oppressed. Here is only ripeness, the fruit of the ages. Enter in.

Come with your broken dreams and burned lives. Enter with your polka-dotted pretenses, to-do lists, and accolades. Rest the stretch marks of success on your soul.

Come with all your lofty complaints and excuses, lengthy dissertations on the world's unfairness. Come with your doubts and fears, apathy and indifferences.

Bring it all.

Come with your disbelief, scientific conclusions and phenomenal reasoning. Come with your world experience, your traveling shoes that have seen too much to hold God in a box.

Just come. Grace can hold all of you.

Come to me, all who are weary,
and I will give you rest.

Matthew 11:28

Soul Stretch

Thank yourself for coming on this journey with me. That is your only task for today. To rest in the fact you chose to show up. We are grateful for you.

2. To Be Enough

You were simply not made to do it all.
Children of Adam,
return to the garden.
Lay yourself down in the moss to rest.
Lure the hourglass to pass you by.
Let the trees whispers their secrets.
Let the evergreens cover your stillness.

Children of Adam, rise up from the dirt.

You were not made to do it all.
Simply, you are enough.

Pray to the Lord for we have had enough
fire and hail. I will let you go.
You don't have to stay any longer.

Exodus 9:28

Soul Stretch

Read the last two lines of this poem to yourself
until you believe it.

You were not made to do it all.
Simply, you are enough.

And if you can't believe it, that too is enough.
Be gentle with wherever you are.

3. To Be With Yourself

To fly away
is to bring you along.

Sacred stillness,
forever with me.

Quiet moment,
the rise of not knowing yet,
paired with knowing
the later ending is yours.

I will listen to your story,
the sound where suffering
and celebration
exists beyond language.

Deny me not my
purpose.
My list is long,
yet still I kneel.

Be still and know that I am God.

Psalm 46:10

Soul Stretch

Find a safe space to sit or lay down. Let yourself just be in the silence, despite all that creeps into your mind. See your thoughts and watch them pass.
Let the silence be your prayer.

4. In Praise of Beauty

Fall's seasonal red carpet,
boasting exotic fashions,
spotlights of flirtatious winks,
descending star-filled stairs.
Shimmering earrings dangle.
Jewels esteem more jewels.

Indeed, it is a noble task
to believe that you are beautiful.

Meanwhile, Earth is stunned in its natural pose,
lifting its face from a holy foundation,
warm complexion of mercy,
forests with unspeakable foliage
boasting color with unbashful leaves,
hallowed ground of heaven's harvest
where spotlights never dull.
Blue sky scraping out the clouds,
the painting of our lifetime.

Notice what you notice.
Praise what should be praised.

From Zion, perfect in beauty, God shines forth.

Psalm 50:2

Soul Stretch

Wear something unnecessary and beautiful today – your favorite earrings, your best shoes, your smile. Let yourself radiate.

5. Finding the Romance

Fresh fallen snow:
the sultry of winter
spreads like a royal tablecloth.

Snowflakes collapse
an epidemic of white spots
drape landscapes in royal grins.

Crystal balls
kiss the ground.

Earth disrobes without shame,
her spirit blushes.
She waits like a bride at the altar
to be touched,
seduced by splendor.

Nature stands naked before Him.
Both blush as they are touched.

Let him kiss me with the kisses of his mouth,
for your love is more delightful than wine.

Song of Songs 1:2

Soul Stretch

Fall in love with something new today.
Let yourself feel pure passion.
Enjoy the rush.
All yourself to blush.

6. Following Mystery

From morning yawn to rising sun,
freckles of stars fade
sandwiched between past, present.
The moon removes its glove.
Constellations of stars gain luster.
Messengers of night massage our dreams.

The glowing handshake of morning
yields its open palm.
Stars unleash their song.
Swizzles of light press on my soul.
Into the mystery, press on!

Beyond all question, the mystery from which true godliness springs is great: He appeared in the flesh, was vindicated by the Spirit, was seen by the angels, was preached among the nations, was believed on in the world, and was taken up in glory.

I Timothy 3:16

Soul Stretch

Make it a point today to watch the sunrise or sunset. Let yourself do nothing but take it its mystery. Stand in awe. Feel the glory. That is all.

7. To play

Youth is an orchard,
and old age a recess.

Both run unleashed
with holy hands,
tumbling fast and free
with impulse and choice,
the heart's true adhesive.

Where are you going,
says the lilac to the bloom?
To the sweet spot of amens,
the innocence of first love.

The flowers are alive.
Above the dirt are the puddles for recess.
Such calm and delight
are worth a thousand hallelujahs.

For all the promises of God find their yes in Him. That is why it is through Him that we utter our amen to God for His glory.

2 Corinthians 1:20

Soul Stretch

What can you say yes to today that will make you come alive? Say yes and dive in. You are never too young or old to play.

8. On Friendship

Friendship offers the possibility
that encourages the soul
to flower
amidst the dark soil.

Friendship offers the possibility
of silence, refreshing
the heart from noisemakers,
the champions of doubt.

Friendship offers the possibility
to share your life,
the millions of moments
of miracles
one being you.

Greater love has no one than this:
to lay down one's life for one's friends.

John 15:13

Soul Stretch

How can you be a miracle to someone today?

9. Taste and See

So much is gleaned
over grilled cheese sandwiches
and French fries
beside the spring wheelbarrow.

The spotlight travels
from winter
as I devour strawberries
beside the creek.

April has come.
Who knows if tomorrow
the pastry will be doused with cinnamon,
or if ice cream will be sold at the stand?

Either way, the tablecloth is set.
I eat in old age what I ate in my youth.

So much to do and so little time,
yet through it all
you are my God.
All life's flavors are delicious.

Taste and see that the Lord is good.
Blessed is the one who takes refuge in Him.

Psalm 34:8

Soul Stretch

Indulge in a food you normally ban yourself from. Many people give up a food for Lent and if you are doing that, we applaud you. But let yourself taste something exotic today that perhaps you haven't eaten since childhood – a lollipop, a candy necklace, grass from your yard. Let yourself return to the place where your taste buds danced.

10. Embracing the Beyond

Under heaven's blanket
flicker our night lights
strung from ocean to ocean
without power or fear.

How do these bulbs hang in
perfect formation?
Do they wait in limbo to shine
or dance where they are placed?

City of stars,
you defy our aloneness.
Flickering lanterns,
you make us ache in desire
to behold the brightest of you.
You pull back the curtain
to reveal that
all light is strung
has a source.

He determines the number of the stars
and calls them each by name.

Psalm 147:4

Soul Stretch

If your night sky affords you,
make the stars your prayerspace. Count them.
Follow their patterns.
Let yourself feel small in their embrace.

11. To Passion

Here I stand, trying to walk directly, attempting temperance, feigning adulthood. *I will choose rationally, wisely, orderly,* I tell myself.

Yet you stand knocking, thirsty. Insistent, I pause at the sprawling crossroad of logic and heart, and you seek to vanish the paradox. I look for reason and you point to my gut. I ask for a whisper and on the horizon, a flashing bolt trembles.

How predominantly fashionable of you.

You pursue me like the Renaissance pursued the painter. Ever capable of poetry, luring with dramatic props of excellence.

Long ago I abandoned the turbulent cloisters for more sophisticated driftwood. I forsook the drama in exchange for a more temperate communion. But you call and ask me to ravage a meal. Yoke me not with this burden of passion.

I shut the shade. Outside, the knocking continues, slow and steady. Oh soul, do not answer the door. To awake to passion is to change everything. I would give you my veins to silence your revelation, but my life is exactly what you desire.

I slept but my heart was awake. Listen! My beloved is knocking: "Open to me, my sister, my darling, my dove, my flawless one. My head is drenched with dew, my hair with the dampness of the night."

Song of Songs 5:2

Soul Stretch

What are you most afraid to feel passionate about, fearful that your expectations will be dashed should you dare to hope for it? Let the things that scares you knock on your heart today. Let yourself imagine it as a guest at your dinner table. Invite her in.

12. Return to Belief

Brevity of innocence,
the pacifier of childhood.

Within a child's heart
are lullabies of wonder.
Nightingales sing their
bedtime songs.
A child believes
these little birds float.

Yet soon we grow
wiser then a flower.
Overlooking the moon,
we wean ourselves
from teepees and coddles.
Forgetting to trace
the fingers of the Creator,
we chronicle heaven a fairy tale.

We forget to trust that
we are part of the story.

Let the children come to me and do not hinder them, but to such belong the kingdom of God. Truly, truly I say to you, whoever does not receive the kingdom of God like a child shall not enter it.

Luke 18:16-17

Soul Stretch

Draw a picture of yourself as a child. Include the people and activities that you loved. Add in all your passions. Hang it on the refrigerator and be proud of all you once knew to be true.

13. Prayer

Prayer argues through the silence
dismantling thoughts,
unmuzzling jaws,
wanting to be hear.

Still we shut our mouths
and talk to no one.

We are the enemy of our own petitions
living without confession or repentance
believing that everything
will work out
with or without prayer.

It's time to start a conversation.

Therefore confess your sins to one another
and pray for one another,
that you may be healed.
The prayer of a righteous person
Has great power as it is working.

James 5:18

Soul Stretch

What have you been afraid to pray about? What have you been avoiding, too afraid to ask for, to afraid to face? Sit with that today and let silence be your prayer.

14. To Listen

God speaks to hearts
that feel varnished
polishing us in and out of season.

God speaks to children
in dreams,
small voices of tiny prayers.

God breaks up the ground
for daffodils,
unfolding their petals of innocence.

God whispers to trees
to root
and to not whisper the secrets of soil.

God speaks to midnight
of chivalry
on nights when the stars fail to shine.

God speaks of himself
through seasons
that we may know He is God.

The Spirit himself bears witness with our spirit
that we are children of God.

Romans 8:16

Soul Stretch

How much of your prayer life is listening? Take a few moments to go outside today and sit somewhere in nature. Look for signs that God is near you. Pay attention to any signs that the seasons are changing, the buds are growing, and that life is moving forward.

15. Learn from Nature

Tell everyone the creek overflows
with abundant ripples of ideas.
Waters flow as rapids
shaping our dreams with vision.

The fawn loses its spots.
Butterflies spread their wings.
All things in motion
beside the riverbed
sculpting humanity's heart.

Believe in the divine currents
that flip the mundane to extraordinary.
Each polished rock
a stepping stone:
our amazing graces.

Whoever believes in me, as Scripture has said, rivers of living water will flow from within them.

John 7:38

Soul Stretch

In your travels today, find a small pebble or stone. Place it on your kitchen countertop or windowsill, somewhere where you will see it often during Lent. Each time you see it, remind yourself of this: You are loved. You are being polished. You are beautiful.

16. Worship

The ancient shade draws up its curtain
flooding the eyes with light.
The knocking continues slow, steady,
the lure of creation alive.

Trees clap in worship
Mountains bow in awe.
Whale and sea lion kneel
without hands or feet.

Gravitational templates of creativity.
Invitational pleasures to marvel.
The unconfined freedom of cliff, peak,
sky and air,
God's chandeliers on earth
from which we swing.

Lift your incredible faces
to this glory-filled delights.
With jubilant crimson smiles
wave petals of praise.

You will go out in joy and be led forth in peace; the mountains and hills will burst into song before you, and all the trees of the field will clap their hands.

Isaiah 55:12

Soul Stretch

Spend today writing down a list of everything you are grateful for. Let your heart rest in gratitude. Revel in all that is good around you.

17. Music of Praise

Oh my soul,
gestation of my mother,
weightless orb of refuge
fusing head to heart
mingling mind and spirit,
you are my capsule to eternity.

Instrument of spiritual pitch
composition of my dreams
orchestrate inspiration
in the deep chambers of me.
Ensemble every note
in harmonious faith.
Praise the Lord!

Bless the Lord , O my soul!
Praise the Lord!

Psalm 104:35

Soul Stretch

Turn on your favorite music that lifts your heart to praise. Sing loudly. Sing softly. Simply, let yourself sing. No one is watching, but Someone is listening. I promise.

18. I Don’t Know How

I don't know how to praise.

Somedays it seems that God has
cut the cord of humanity,
remains seated on a birthing stool,
and fails to write in the margins of eternity.

Somedays, my faith is stillborn.

Little twig heart.
That is all I have.
Sprigs of unmet passion,
growing behind the barn,
handpicked and gathered.

I am a little bouquet
waiting to be picked.

I don't know how to
fill in the gaps or
fill the baskets with flowers.

When my spirit grows faint within me,
it is you who watch over my way.

Psalm 142:3

Soul Stretch

The last few days have been focused on praise and gratitude. But perhaps that's been difficult. Maybe your life hasn't felt very joyful and maybe you don't know how to find your way back. That is okay too. Today is the day to let yourself say, "I don't know how." You can fill in the blank after. I don't know how to _______. This is the bravest starting place yet.

19. Discovery

A return to the prayer closet.

A yielding from knee and heart.

Undusting my words
trusting my process
lifting my palms in surrender again.

Herein lies the discovery.

Return to your rest, my soul,
for the Lord has been good to you.

Psalm 116:7

Soul Stretch

Return today to wherever it is where you feel most able to pray. Stay there for awhile, praying in whatever way feels most natural. If that is through song, sing. If you need to paint your prayers, paint. Journal, scribble, doodle, sit. Either way, return.

20. To Grieve

Linger awhile more and peer upon what is passing. Drink deep the tears. Swallow, digest, and remain seated at the table of mourning. Do not quickly remove your shoes nor believe what cannot be heard. What is around you is within you. Poets know that poetry is not written in the daylight, but resounds in the dark. The dark is the rebuilder of your nest.

That which makes us hollow makes us fly.

Let your tears become your hallowed ground. Hold on, sparrow. Morning will dawn. So too, weeping will cease. But for now, let sorrow hail. Fling wide your empty arms and faithless chatter. This too is hallowed ground. It is where we cry the most, and hope the least, that our wings are made strong.

Lay to rest, little sparrow. Your voice is whispered in the halls of light. Winds, let this moment pass. Oh little one, your greatest work is ahead, not behind. Hold on.

And even now, amidst despair, do you not know you are a hero?

Hope deferred makes the heart sick,
but a longing fulfilled is a tree of life.

Proverbs 13:12

Soul Stretch

Sometimes a return to prayer is also a return to disappointment. Sometimes it's a reminder of all that we have lost and all that we still hope for. Expectation is difficult and loss is painful.

21. To Weep

Be faithful in weeping.
Let your droplets caress your flushed cheeks
and do not be afraid.
Weak and broken wing,
it is time to be frail.
Let someone else harvest the worm.
Let another bring in the twig.

Your task is allowing all that is in you to seep.

Swelling eyelids, fear not thy explosion.
Fling your voice as a tattered cloth.
Let all your prayers demand answers to questions.

How can we awake yet dream?
How can love be lonely?
Do miracles ever exist?

Linger. Peer. Stamp out all that is unfair.
Mourn all innocence lost.

For now, morning is broken. So too is the moment.

Indeed, the stars have lost their points
and North is no longer true.

The Holy is in the weeping.

The hearts of the people cry out to the Lord. You walls of Daughter Zion, let your tears flow like a river day and night; give yourself no relief, your eyes no rest.

Lamentations 2:18

Soul Stretch

I'm not going to mandate you to tears, but hey – if a good cry is in order, put on that sappy music, turn on "The Notebook," or call that friend that always listens. Give yourself permission to let grief out. If you try to keep it in, it will only hold you captive longer.

22. The Practice of Honesty

If Holiness is unfair
and God is a recluse,
if we are left alone in the world
to cliff-hang on doubt
swinging on chandeliers of pain,
if all that is sacred is false
because we have looked honestly at the world,
if God hears our prayers
but does not respond,
this teasing is extraordinary.
Our soul awakens in these momentary rants.
To these I write.

My God, my God, why have you forsaken me?
Why are you so far from saving me,
so far from my cries of anguish?

Psalm 22:1

Soul Stretch

Have an honest conversation with God. Tell him all your disappointments. Tell him all your sorrows. Don't hold back a complaint. Today, give yourself permission to be honest, even if you think you sound whiny. It's a rant day. Trust me, it's good for you. God can handle it.

23. Pain and Pleasure

Beyond that, I hear your questions:

Does He find pleasure in our dangling,
looking at his children as they cling
like drabs of clay to broken leaves?
Why does he hang humanity out to dry?
What is with this God who finds
gain in our weariness?
And from there, we hear of pleasure?

Sea-reef heart, half-bent from
the wind's torn sail, take notice.
Oh large mass of men and women
slanting towards mercy, take heart.

Pleasure is our natural slant.
Jagged thread, hold on!
For who can bargain with the moon
or reach for it?
Little thog of clay, cease your crumbling.
Lay down.
Rest.
The pastures are thick with green and await you.

Those who sow with tears
will reap with songs of joy.

Psalm 126:5

Soul Stretch

After your rant, let yourself be with whatever comes. If you need to rant more, today is the day for it. If you need to rest, do that. Do a little self-care, even if just for a few minutes. It's okay to feel both pleasure and pain in the same moment.

24. To Stop Doing

Deep in your belly a conversation brews, but is quickly silenced. All you should be doing pulls at you. If only you had more to give. For a second, you disrobe these jabs, but elsewhere hands are pulling, gasping for your attention.

The list of causes to join are endless. Inside, your stomach curls, as outside your cheeks lose their rosy flush.

But your honor is not found in paleness.

You were not made to do it all. You were simply made.

Turn toward your life. Stop running towards martyrdom, cloaking yourself with ribbons that will later choke you. Pause. Say no.

My sacrifice, O God, is a broken spirit.
A broken and contrite heart you will not despise.

Psalm 51:17

Soul Stretch

Today is a day to practice saying NO. Rather than doing more, try doing less. Take a day to ignore your laundry. Take a night off from making an extra fabulous meal. Find something little that normally brings you guilt and ignore it. Let yourself rest.

25. Instead, When You Wake

Before your mangled toes grace the ground, notice what becomes you. Imprint what curls the edges of your lips. And do more of that.

It doesn't interest me if you can save the whole world but lose your own hope. Put on a silk robe. I know what you say. This is not the path of the divine. Even God did not spare his own son from the claw. Is not sacrifice not the only purpose?

To that, I say, who made your cheeks to blush? Even the Christ trusted God to restore life. How can we do less?

For purpose does not only arrive in a package of pain. The light in your eyes opens the eyelids of others. Keep coming alive.

The precepts of the Lord are right,
giving joy to the heart.
The commands of the Lord are radiant,
giving light to the eyes.

Psalm 19:8

Soul Stretch

Today is a day for a bathrobe or something extra fuzzy. Put on your most comfortable clothes as soon as you wake or right before bed. Enjoy the soft edges of life.

26. Thirst

You will return from where you are sent.
You will feed the sparrow there
and cup your hand with water.
You will subdue the lion
and feed on bone and marrow.
You will be asked to remain.
You will write lyrics exposing your doubt.
You will unbite your lip.
You will spew discontent
and your breast will be uncovered.
You will be asked to remain.

Yet I will not leave you in drought forever.
You will carry a bucket beside you
and it will be filled with water.

The desert and the parched land will be glad.
The wilderness will rejoice and blossom.

Isaiah 35:1

Soul Stretch

Carry a water bottle with you today.
Every time you feel stress today,
take a large sip and close your eyes.
Remind yourself there is water to sustain you,
inside and out.

27. Finding the Impossible

He finds us in bondage
dislodging the chains,
reversing confusion.

He sees our oppression
feeding our poverty
giving movement to paralyzed hope.

He listens to sterile faith
hearing our plastic prayers
and babbles of pride.

He whispers in our inner chamber
the pulp of our heart
that love is the pathway to freedom.

When the Lord restored the fortunes of Zion,
we were like those who dreamed.

Psalm 126:1

Soul Stretch

Wherever you are in your own Lenten journey – in confusion, in bliss, in doubt, in disbelief – let yourself try out one impossible thing. If you've never run a mile, try it today. If you've never eaten okra, fry it up. Do something that has always seemed impossible today and see if, just maybe, the possibilities are actually closer than you think.

28. On Joy

Joy always comes. It comes with or without us, ambitious, blind babes that we are, flooding the noonday with light.

As adults, we are born premature, eyes half closed. We must be held and weighed, carried close to arms larger than our own. There we rest. There, we feel the heaviness around us that falls prey to a broken spirit. But in His arms, we find a place. Here, our muscles grow. Tendons heal. Vision welcomes. And all that is old becomes new.

In the beginning, God speaks. God speaks and swamps dry out. God speaks and hermits come forth in pairs. God speaks and sadness cracks open stone. God speaks and the land bursts with morning dew, moon, stars, and galaxies. God speaks and all becomes innocent again, including us.

Joy comes like the droplet. In small, shiny cases. In the morning, once the night has been conquered, there is a scent of hope. In small tiny ways, we gather small tiny dewdrops. We learn to drink, gawk, to know and be known.

And then, we learn to sing. The forests await our melody. The world has bid us come.

They will enter Zion with singing. Everlasting joy will crown their heads. Gladness and joy will overtake them, and sorrow and sighing will flee away.

Isaiah 35:10

Soul Stretch

To find joy today, let yourself return to the state of a child. Find a friend or a partner and ask them for a hug. A good, long hug. Let yourself feel their arms around you, melting you, revitalizing your strength.

29. Waiting

Unanswered pleas
circle the sky.
All of them worthy
of divine intervention.
The enter the heavens as
mutant vapors
songs without wings
a pattern of cries
falling on deaf ears.

Silence is the prism of prayer.

Through the hush
the crystals wait,
reflectors of light
turn prayers on ourselves
asking why and what we seek.

And still we wait.

But those who hope in the Lord will renew their strength. They will soar on wings like eagles; they will run and not grow weary, they will walk and not be faint.

Isaiah 40:31

Soul Stretch

Patience is my least favorite spiritual virtue. Waiting is my bane, particularly when it's something important. Today is a day to practice it intentionally. If you are at the grocery store, let someone in front of you. If you are driving, take the slow lane. Do something intentionally that makes you wait an extra few minutes and notice if any positive outcome shows up because of your slowness.

30. Embracing Imperfection

Zone of uncertainty
with my belly bloat and skinny jeans,
designer labels of religion
are not my size!

I leisurely delight
on fashion and fame,
but diet fads starve my soul.

I will delight in the lantern of heaven
and his gorgeous fabric of grace,
the stained red carpet
of a blood soaked cross
that resizes my soul
reshapes my image
until I delight in myself
as He delights in me.

For God was pleased to have all his fullness dwell in him and through him to reconcile to himself all things, whether things on earth or things in heaven, by making peace through his blood, shed on the cross.

Colossians 1:19-20

Soul Stretch

Wabi-sabi is a traditional Japanese notion that believes beauty is found in imperfection. This Japanese aesthetic honors the natural, rough, incomplete, and imperfect parts of beauty that we so often forget. This is most exemplified in Japanese flower arrangements, bonsai trees, or in Japanese pottery. Today, try to practice wabi-sabi. Use your cracked mug for your coffee cup. Wear a shirt that's has small rip (in an acceptable place). Dawn your favorite over-worn and dying shoes. Embrace imperfection and the beauty of the well-loved. All things have reconciled and made new.

31. Asking Forgiveness

Intimate as honey and spoon
are repentance and faith.

Convictions carve rivulets
into hearts,
spritzing riverbanks
of apology.

Intimacy surges,
the current of the Almighty
flooding the soul
with living water
so the heart can speak and believe.

Upstream, downstream
flowing spritzes of grace
thawing iceburgs of resistance.
When we forgive, we are free,
our soul cascaded to life.

Therefore confess your sins to each other and pray for each other so that you may be healed. The prayer of a righteous person is powerful and effective.

James 5:16

Soul Stretch

Speaking of embracing imperfection, it's okay to embrace our own shortcomings. No one is perfect so it's okay not to pretend that you are. Pretending only makes you look weird. Ask forgiveness today from someone who may need to hear it from you. Say the "I'm sorry" you've been dreading. There's no one to free but yourself.

32. Releasing Bitterness

Rainforest of heaven
this is your purpose:
cultivating passion
sprucing hearts to thrive.

Eden of blooms
grow compassion and love.
Gardens of flowers
pollinating faith.

Yet bitter roots dig deep.
Weeds creep in.
Brambles and tangles,
thistles and spades,
spiritual foliage
crushing and rubbing
our wounds,
telling us to cling to hurts.

Which will win?
The weeds or the soul?
Even the dandelions can entice.
Bitterness has its beauty.
Choose what you will cultivate.

Get rid of all bitterness, rage and anger, brawling and slander, along with every form of malice.

Ephesians 4:31

Soul Stretch

Today is a day to write down the name of someone you feel bitter about. Maybe they have wronged you. Maybe they've broken your trust. Take a scrap of paper and write their name on it. Put the paper in your pocket and every time you come across it throughout the day, ask God to help you release your bitterness toward them. It's one small step on a long journey of release, but it can start today.

33. Grace

Countless rituals
cannot purify,
cleanse,
deodorize our hearts.

Concealment
devours the soul.
Secrecy is never satisfied
as toxins of pride spread.

Holy spirit scrubs, soaks,
sanitizes, sanctifies.
Rinse with living water.

Would not God have discovered it,
since he knows the secrets of the heart?

Psalm 44:21

Soul Stretch

When we were little, we loved sharing secrets with our friends. As adults, we still love having someone to confide in, yet our secrets may seem more weighty. Tell someone today something you've been afraid to share. It can be a positive piece of news or something you've been hiding, but get it off your chest. I promise you will feel better having done so.

34. Spiritual Fragrance

Aftershave of grace
that perfumes the heart
with scent of the Almighty.
Aromas of holiness,
burn within the heart's lamp.
Praise, worship.

Altar burning with sacrifice.
A wick cut short
by sticks of hate.
Angelic motorcades
and heaven's podium
remain silent.
No convoy came to his assistance.
His death became eternal incense.
He spread his life into the ground.

Spiritual fragrances of heart,
proceed in word and deed.
Raise the torch
to banish tidiness to holiness,
a wick of faith
that burns into forever.

But thanks be to God, who in Christ always leads us in triumphant procession, and through us spreads the fragrance of the knowledge of him everywhere."
2 Corinthians 2:14

Soul Stretch

If you were a perfume maker, what would grace smell like? Would it be a clean, fresh scent like rain or a beautiful bouquet of flowers? Would it be musky, holding scents of the spice that brought us here? Put on a fragrance today that smells like grace to you. Remind yourself, every time you smell it, that grace is all around.

35. Practicing Gratitude

The world will swallow memos
from angelic palms in flight.
It will mask spiritual oils from above
that are constantly surrounding.

The world will shrink the fonts
of heaven's etchings,
hiding havens where cherubs
try to nestle us in grace.

The world will peppercorn faith,
block our view of innocence and paradise.

From mud huts
the villagers can see more clearly.
They grasp each other's hands
and find Him who cleans the dirt.

From dust to pulse,
the waltz begins.
Each breath invites another trust.
Each breath asks us to say thank you.

You are a hiding place for me;
you preserve me from trouble;
You surround me with shouts of deliverance.

Psalm 32:7

Soul Stretch

What do you take most for granted? Your family, your health, your home? Where is it most easy to complain and miss all the goodness around you? Make a point to notice what you most ignore and say thank you today.

36. Welcoming Seasons

Poppies gain momentum.
The soil shows signs of survival.
Between the shadows
and chandeliers,
I look out my bedroom
window at bloom,
past giving life to present.

I disrobe my bedroom linens
and put all winter clothes out to dry.

Spring has come.
Hide no more under all that
winter has spread.

Poetry and poppies.
Chandeliers and shadows.
Choose good over evil.
The shadows have left.

There is a time for everything
and a season for every activity
under heaven.

Ecclesiastes 3:1

Soul Stretch

Put away something that reminds you of winter today and put out something that reminds you of spring. Maybe it's time to retire the down coat to the attic or decorate with tulips. Either way, welcome the change of seasons and the freshness it brings.

37. Foot Washing

Her feet are barren.
Thongs of clay
straddling compromise.

Her pores full of loneliness.
Her skin full of scars.

Scramble to attention,
all who see her here.
Surrender to her pedicure
and welcome her dirt.
Learn from her journey
and let her take you in.

This is the spa of humanity.

When he had finished washing their feet, he put on his clothes and returned to his place. "Do you understand what I have done for you?" he asked them.

John 13:12

Soul Stretch

On Maundy Thursday, we remember the Last Supper of Christ and this foot washing ceremony. It's very humbling to wash someone's feet. If you have a partner or friend who lives with you, swap foot washes tonight. If you don't, offer to do something for others today that is beyond your comfort zone. Receive the blessing that comes from serving others in ways you normally don't.

38. Good Friday

Jolts of conviction shift a pause and
the conversation begins.
There were no whispers, only shouts,
splintering flesh.
The cross flayed,
and he was no more.

Swelling eyelids
for the shaving of Christ.
Blood stained confetti covers the streets.
A tree toppled, plucked from earth.
Vocal chords sputtered.
Mangled hearts graced our homeland.

The tourniquets of grace.

Weak broken wings,
what is fractured cannot fly.

We share blood-soaked grief,
but if we stay seated
at the table of mourning,
bones collect strength.
Jagged hope, hang on!
For tomorrow his love
will return.

For if while we were enemies
we were reconciled to God by the death
of His Son, much more, now that we are reconciled ,
Shall we be saved by His life.

Romans 5:10

Soul Stretch

Spend a moment pondering your own spiritual history.
Where have you felt closest to God?
When have you felt most distant?
Where has your own Good Friday been, the day
when you are sure that God has died and you are alone.
What has brought the resurrection?

39. To Anoint

One morning, I anointed a fruit fly. I did not mean to start this way. I stood in my kitchen, peeling apples, trying to pray effectually, as I carved away the flesh of the fruit. Empty skins fell out of my hands, and my indifference peeled away with the rough edges. I carved. I prayed.

Then a fly landed.

I ignored him and kept folding in the dough, crumbling the flour into my hands along with the shortening. Kneed the dough, try not to crumble, attempt to be present.

Peels grew upon peels until my kitchen was a multitude of discarded skins. Juice pouring out of fruit, slices of layered compassion, love, and goodness to all creatures.

Except the fruit fly that kept landing on my arm . He was not part of the blessing. Him, I despised. Him, who disrupted my baking and disrupted my prayers. I slammed the knife in his direction.

I missed and cut myself.

It's hard to intercede when you are bleeding.

But I tell you, love your enemies
and pray for those who persecute you.

Matthew 5:44

Soul Stretch

The hardest work is loving those that annoy you.
This is the real work of Lent.
Loving those who we don't understand.
Loving ourselves when we aren't our best.
Loving God when we can't comprehend Him.
Today, do something loving for someone
or something that you can't stand.
This is the power of grace.

40. To Anoint (Cont'd)

All I want to do is scream and scrape from the bottom of the bowl all that is tainted, soured, and now crusted. All I want to do is give up. Instead, I wash my hands, apply a Band-Aid, and kneed the dough.

I look to my left, and the fruit fly is covered with olive oil. It has taken a bath in my Crisco mix.

How can I pray when a fly is in my food? And after I cut myself?

In the next room, I heard a call to the dinner table – an invitation to sit and feast, to say simple prayers of thanks.

More time passed. The fly stood in the Crisco. In the next room, I heard children ask for seconds and thirds, giggling over the pies.

And then, I realized the sticky fly was my prayer. Dear God, I hate the fly, but help me to love all I hate - including the crust of humanity.

The fly resurrected and flew away from the oil. This is where the work begins – blessing flies, bringing nourishment to bones and body, and eventually sitting down from toiling and enjoying the feast.

People will come from east and west
and north and south and take their places
at the feast in the kingdom of God.

Luke 13:29

Soul Stretch

Welcome to the last day of Lent.
You have completed 40 days of soul stretches.
It is now time to feast.
Keep praying throughout your days,
from your kitchens to your cars.
Let your toil cease.
Know you are loved.
Simply, you are enough.

THANK YOU

To my dearest girlfriends – Lynne, Elva, Peggy – for always believing in me. I love you.

To my daughters for always loving me.

To my husband for providing for me.

To God for listening to my rants.

To my readers for reading along with me.

Thank you.

Love,
Linda

ABOUT THE AUTHOR

Linda Strube is a mother of 4, grandmother of 8,
and great-grandmother of 1. She loves cozying up by the
fireplace during snowstorms, baking apple pies, taking
prayer walks in the fall woods, reading, and drawing.
Linda has numerous written books in her adult life,
but it took 70 years to have the courage to publish.
An avid Sunday school teacher, Linda comes most alive
with children. She resides in Pennsylvania with her
husband Ric and their two dogs, Shiloh and Teddy.

Linda getting ready for her daughter
Jennifer's wedding in New Orleans.

64730373R00059

Made in the USA
Middletown, DE
16 February 2018